Fun at the Fair

Written by Narinder Dhami

Illustrated by Arief Putra

Collins

T0337799

"Craig, we are off to the fair!" his dad said.

"Grab a jumper, Craig," Ranjeeta said. "It is freezing out."

Ranjeeta was dad's partner and Scarlet's mum.

Scarlet scampered downstairs. "Craig, I need you to see this!" she blurted out.

"Look at the Monster Coaster, it is so cool!"' she said with glee. Craig blinked and gulped. It looked frightening!

The night was clear, with sparkling silver stars. They joined the crowds.

Scarlet grabbed Craig. "Quick, quick! Let's get on the Monster Coaster! It's the biggest thrill at the fair!" she exclaimed.

Craig felt a lump in his throat.
"All right," he blurted out.

Scarlet pointed at the Monster Coaster.
"Look at it! I am not afraid!"
she boasted.

They entered the Monster Coaster and sat down in the pink train. The train started to creep along the steel track.

It speeded up and swooped down
a steep hill.

"Fantastic!" Craig exclaimed.

"I am frightened!" Scarlet burst out.

"Do not be afraid, Scarlet," Craig said.
"Grab my hand!"

"Hands in the air is better! Feel the speed!" yelled Craig.

Scarlet and Craig

🐾 Review: After reading 🐾

Use your assessment from hearing the children read to choose any GPCs, words or tricky words that need additional practice.

Read 1: Decoding

- On page 3, point to the word **partner**. Ask: What sort of partner is meant here? Is it a business partner or life partner? (*life*)
- Challenge the children to sound out the names, and then point to the long vowel graphemes in each word.

  Scarlet   **Ranjeeta**   **Mons<u>te</u>r Coas<u>te</u>r**   **Craig**

- Let children work in pairs to take turns to point to a word for the other to sound out in their heads, only reading it aloud when they can do so fluently. Demonstrate first with the group.

Read 2: Prosody

- Turn to pages 8 and 9, and focus on the dialogue.
  - On page 8, discuss how Craig is feeling emotionally and physically. (e.g. *afraid; as if he's got a lump in his throat*) Point to **blurted**. Can the children role-play Craig and blurt out his words?
  - On page 9, point to **boasted**, and ask: What does this tell us about how Scarlet is feeling? (e.g. *confident and clever*). Can the children role-play Scarlet and read her words boastfully?
- Reread the pages as a group, letting the children take turns to read the characters' parts.

Read 3: Comprehension

- Discuss any experiences children have had of funfairs, through stories or real life. Ask: What do you think makes a ride like Monster Coaster scary for some people?
- Focus on the theme of fear.
  - Compare each child's feelings on page 11 with those they had on pages 8 and 9. (*Scarlet is the one who is afraid now, and Craig isn't*)
  - Ask: Why does Scarlet feel less afraid on page 12? (e.g. *Craig is holding her hand*)
- Look together at pages 14 and 15. Ask the children to use the pictures to help them retell the story in their own words.